The Giddings

*There were many travellers ... who, posting along that highway,
would turn aside to break their journey*

A.L.Maycock

John Greening

The Giddings
published in the United Kingdom in 2021
by Mica Press

c/o Leslie Bell
47 Belle Vue Road, Wivenhoe, Colchester, Essex CO7 9LD
www.micapress.co.uk | books@micapress.co.uk

ISBN 978-1-869848-28-6

Text copyright © 2021 John Greening
Illustrations copyright © 2021 Rosie Greening

The rights of John Greening and Rosie Greening to be identified as the author and illustrator respectively of this work have been asserted by him and her in accordance with the Copyright, Designs and Patents Act of 1988.

All rights reserved.

To my friend Stuart Henson, who came this way earlier.

Argument

An unnamed man from our own day finds himself not far from Little Gidding, site of Nicholas Ferrar's seventeenth-century spiritual community, and feels a strange urge to make the pilgrimage. Walking there, he hears the trees addressing him – an ash near Molesworth, where cruise missiles were wheeled out in the 1980s; one of Huntingdonshire's surviving elms; a rare black poplar at the wildlife centre; and as he approaches the Giddings (Great, Steeple and Little), shadowed by wind-power, a hawthorn and an elder. At Little Gidding itself he is met by a conflagration, a reminder that one of the last things Nicholas Ferrar did was order the burning of his books in front of the church (adding to speculation that he was a witch). The trees at this point present their own alternative reading list, before Ferrar steps out of his time and addresses the visitor in a formal canzone, the poem's centre-piece. Things now begin to move rapidly backwards, but first, the local children who in Ferrar's day were paid a penny for every psalm they could learn, are heard singing. As if in some ritual performance, the man sees acted out key scenes from Ferrar's life, beginning with the London plague that brought him to Gidding, while the tree songs continue: oak, sycamore, sweet chestnut, pine, lime. These are interleaved with brief prose sketches of his involvement with American colonies, his walk through Spain, his stay in Italy, and earlier still his engagement as a courtier for a royal visit to the Low Countries. Finally, he is back at Cambridge, a student. The trees are seen dancing, and there is a concluding dialogue between birch and yew. Our man sets off back to his Travelodge.

This was not the time to be going anywhere. The weather was foul and it had been a long drive. His staff were exhausted. They had found a half decent Travelodge off the A1, and thoughts were turning to steaks and drinks and falling asleep to a hundred channels of TV. But as they were driving in he saw across the slip-road, through the blurry windscreen, a very old sign, *To the Giddings*, and he knew immediately that he must go there. The rain had stopped, but the wind was getting up. Waving to his secretary as if he were nipping out for a smoke, he walked over to the sign, headed off into the dark, and is now thoroughly lost. The shadowy mass in front of him he is almost certain must belong to Monks Wood. He can hear the restless roar of its boughs, but in particular the distinctive rattle of a huge ash tree, silhouetted against the one patch of light in the sky. Since it's the only familiar thing, reminding him of his childhood ash, of hiding inside its hollow, Roundheads and Cavaliers, of pushing himself right through in the hope of magicking the misery away, he moves towards it, listening.

Between close rings, inaccessibly, in this bunch
of keys, we keep our secret: how they used to pull
the World's End on its twelve giant trailer tyres along
Huntingdonshire lanes as if ready to launch.

But they were only taking the night air, with bats
and owls, check-checking their hunting skills, the same air
we harmlessly exhaled and never thought to fear,
when all we knew of dieback was that rainfall hurts.

Those convoys sidling from their perimeter gate
would hardly have noticed our ditch, or ever heard
that such arcane and ancient forces might be wired
(though souls at Gidding knew) into each dull black bud.

It's a familiar sound, the rattle of ash twigs. But he has to move on, up and over the low hill. There is a glow on the other side of the wold, arc-lights, perhaps, but he doesn't want to go towards them. There's something else. He leaves Monks Wood behind him and follows the road. Bare fields, with scrappy hedgerows, chiefly elm shoots still pushing up and dreaming of the heights they had achieved in the 1970s, but never reaching beyond twenty or thirty feet. Yet here is one that seems to be defying that rule. It calls him over.

It's not only when you see me shedding my tufted foliage
that you might think, *melancholy tree.* I am also for coffins.
In fact, there is enough of gloom about my very name to make
elm hateth man and waiteth true.

But you know the one thing people know about me, if anything,
those older, at least, with thicker trunks, who've lived through storms,
                                                  though less
the young who find when they come it isn't dendrology that moves
their mouths and bodies like green boughs.

The English Elm, and ah, quite dead, except in certain paintings by
Constable & co., who never dreamt it might change, and went on *dip,
dip, dip* until they also died. You see we all become extinct,
not just the precious landscape trees.

We could not make coffins enough for them, the religious zealots
and atheists, the dancers and pontificators, all vanish
from the landscape. As you will, with your over-eager business card
made out of American pulp.

And so will the wheelwright and the millwright who were that much in love
with the Wych Elm they failed to see which way the wind was blowing that
blew them out of the picture where their wheels and stones go rolling on
down into your oblivion.

And so will the makers of scantlings, felloes, Indian clubs, pales,
skirtings, nosings, chamfers and mouldings, along with their very words,
running away in a water-pipe made of us into a butt
of a joke which is also us.

You are asking what became of the community. What became
of mine? You see a few of them, piteous, with drips at their trunks,
or hear of one left stranded; no, a thousand thousand suckers push
up to be heard: *We're English Elm.*

He is feeling tired. A group of buildings rise up beside the road out of sight of the great elm. But he hears it before he sees it. Smells it before even that. Some faint meatiness on the air, a sweetness of old bedding; and now the noises. Birds, not the kind that live in Middle England, not even the no longer exotic red kite (that high insistent cry), but colourful chatterings over the cut fields. Then a snort or snuffle of something more accustomed to roaming other wilder plains, and – unmistakably – a tiger's roar.

Whereas we are of here, and have been
from the start, our cages made of hearts,
and in our heartwood chest we carry
manuscripts of psalms they used to sing
though we remember only *Cut me
green and keep me dry*. We number but
a thousand yet we can raise our voice
above a whisper when there's need, and
'no other native tree can compare'
the man said, whose production of leaves
was above average. Energy
is our theme. We watch the runners pass,
the rowers and racers, and know Zeus
punished that chariot-driver, but
rewarded his siblings by turning
them into us. The lesson is, don't
hurry, lean, whisper, allow yourself
once in a while to lose your head, re-
doubling, re-rooting, harbour your best
resources for the moment you reach
whatever underworld you are now
(in a slow turning of the wind, look)
beginning to descend into, with
hopelessness, but with Hercules too.

The movement draws him away from the wildlife centre, a series of ghostly arms sweeping through the night air, as if a whole school of fundamentalist preachers were standing on the hill exhorting us to believe in renewable energy. Well, he knew a thing or two about renewables, but the sight of this wild creature – wilder than anything they could house at Hamerton – disturbs him. There is a moon rising, and he seems to be at a grand entranceway, a fancy which would have taken him even further from the overgrown gate where he's standing had he not caught his hand on a prickle.

Can I interest you in this?
From the self-same bush left
by Joseph of Arimathea
on Glastonbury Tor?

Or one of these, so that you're
ready for May Day when
it comes dancing round (and even here
they can't stop reels and jigs)?

Then perhaps a bunch of twigs
suitable for a torch
to guide you on whatever night path
you're following, good luck?

What about this berry, plucked
from one of the jewels
in King Richard's crown the day he fell
horseless to my cousin?

Your lady-friend, she doesn't
own a thing as fine as
once hung on the maypole in the Strand,
here, look, your last chance to...

at least have a dance or two,
one of the old patterns
in and out of primrose and speedwell,
nothing to stop you here

unless – Jack – you wish to veer
that way, which I would not
point you myself, not any further
towards Little Gidding.

Nothing but a disused windmill, or rather the body of one, stripped of its sails and any risk of ever being moved by the wind, then converted into a home. The security lights are on and the place looks very inviting. But wait, there was just such a conversion marked on the map, work of decades ago – can he really be at Great Gidding? How did that happen? But it's not the mill, it's the small steeple he has spotted below the fully risen moon that tells him now he has almost found what he came for. From the wall of Steeple Gidding's tiny churchyard, an elder reaches out a bony arm to address him.

what ails you

                                                                                             at any one
                                                                       of our branches
                                              drink
                 yourself to health
                                          or bathe
                                                                                    or breathe

                      so say the elder mothers

                      make a pipe
                      and play
                      your way

                      from this corner
                      of the field
                      of skulls

                      be welcome
                      where we may
                      not go

                      reach out
                      you have
                      arrived

             as it was written with our black bark ink
             and sounded by our secret horns in silver

  (fever   colic   gout   scald   dropsy   ulcer   bruise)

                    not a broken king

                      half a man

Smoke. And it's not wood burning. Through orchards and plantations, he approaches the place his vivid dream has brought him to, but it's all smoke. Of the house, the church, the community he can pick out very little. The bonfire begins to reveal its flames, however, and he is able to see what they are feeding on. Books make up the pyramid of this extraordinary pyre, old books of the kind that take longer to catch, so that you can feel their titles screaming for mercy, lettering like neat gold teeth. Yet the heat is such that he can go no closer. He waits in the spinney, with holly, hazel, wild cherry, wild service. 'The master is burning his conjuring books'. He doesn't know where the cry comes from, but as if in reply, the trees begin:

> The book of the holly is glossy and sharp,
> a mass of advice on exterior decor.
>
> The book of the hazel is feeding and fencing.
> The cherry has written the loveliest of books.
>
> The box plans a sequel to *Emma* in which
> there's a picnic at her house with all trees invited.

The book of the wild service tree is on chess,
the juniper's just finished one about gin.

The book of the walnut is set on a farm
where the brains of the nation are secretly gathered.

The field maple's book of short stories is out
though it's only the big maples get the attention.

The sycamore road series keep on appearing,
dark, with a twist, and they won't go away.

The apple is co-writing (due from his small press)
the pear's rhyming slang cyclopedia.

The book of the willow, the book of the cypress,
are tear-jerkers. The larch does light verse.

The high shelves are groaning and creaking as ever
at privet jokes. Pinus and cedrus

are dark mythological books where your dreams
exude meaning and stickiness sells.

The book of the rowan is critical, close
exegesis of what the First Witch says.

The alder has taken small microphones out
on the streets for her book about H_2O.

The book of the blackthorn is only a slim one
but its lines are savage, satirical, blue.

The spindle tree offers you fairy tales
in their unvarnished original state.

The book of the beech is the book of itself.

As the smoke starts to clear, where the book-saqqara has collapsed, some seven feet in front of the church door stands Nicholas Ferrar. The wicket gate between them opens and then closes again. But who moves first it is hard to say. The effect is like someone approaching their reflection in a mirror. The only way to meet him seems to be through the ash of his holocaust.

It is a gift – that you have journeyed here
to find me in my old life's final hours
at this cremation. These travel stories here
were futile dreams. I've learned to overhear
more useful omens as I sleep: this last
phantasma, for example, reached from here
towards a future time, on through the here-
after, where two were standing. One who prays
and one who never has. Therefore I praise
your stepping from that dream to greet me here
prepared to guide me through the fens of new-
fangleness, draining my path. You always knew

That this would be a gate to copses new,
beyond which certain instincts might cohere
and make it clear just what that avenue
of hamadryads whispered. Trees renew
themselves in special ways that could be ours,
in tree prayer, tree psalm, tree hymn. They start anew
each season, as we should. This is a new
testament deep within the heart, the last
unopened book of God. I have spent the last
ten years not seeing it, and now this new
light breaks across us both. Therefore I praise.
And yet there is a troubling truth that preys

On my ease. How could one who never prays,
whose life's a glistening web of all that's new,
a distraction-maze, a constant reapprais-
ing of romances, chances, fancies, praise-
less sneer, cold compliment, and a brief her-
oic moment, how could one such live praise-
worthily with our group where how it prays
is how it knows itself? And how, where hours
are spent in cheerful prayer and psalm as ours
have been, could one whose element is praise,
whose aim is at the spirit first and last,
how could that man survive, how even last

A single hour in your future? At last,
despite all this, we stand here and appraise
each other: who is the shoe, and who the last?
An owl cries in our silence. When I last
inspected I was Ferrar still, no new
appendages. The same fool. Made to last
like a horse-shoe, to be hammered first, and last-
ly moulded for the grisly trot from here
to where our luck decides. So we stand here.
The children sang their psalm for me this last
few minutes: they know this smouldering hour's
a fuse, and soon I'll count by different hours

From those on their sundial. This now is ours
to weigh up. Treat each moment as your last,
we taught them. Savour the natural hours
beneath a stretch of blue we may call ours
before the sun goes when we'll have to praise
its honesty by moonshine. But to keep our-
selves under vague constellations, through hours
exposed to vast uncertainty, when new
dark pressures hold you down, when all you knew
is crushed into a hole of blackness – ours
is time's great challenge, and it's why we're here,
my friend, between the church and tomb, to hear

Our sentence read from all the writers' ashes here-
abouts, their motion purposeless as ours,
unable to distinguish first from last
as they drift to a judgement: let us praise,
if nothing more, all that we are, and knew.

At this, the air is filled with children's voices, coming from all directions it seems. These are the so-called psalm-children.

we are the children who recite
each Sunday for our penny prize
while others read or write the day
we speak it out aloud by heart
and pennies drop into our palms
a hundred voices cry halloo

we know the blessings and the blight
the broken pot the lifted eyes
the heathen's rage the lion's prey
the driven chaff the panting hart
the clap of hands the clash of arms
we know they're worth a penny too

we work – selah! – throughout the night
attending most of all to size
the shortest and the longest pay
the same a psalm-child's keenest art
is keeping focus on those psalms
whose verses will not cripple you

we know the art of scorn and spite
who toughs it out who breaks and cries
the ones who'll stumble on the way
and those who'll freeze before they start
then worst of all the child who charms
for them we soon find things to do

we're out to fight the weekly fight
no pity for this friend who dries
or that one now turned wet and grey
we'll win by instinct or by art
by subtle threat or shrewd alarms
but never let a rival through

*we are the children widow's mite
or farmer's boy we'll claim your eyes
and rather see them boiled than say
today you played the better part
it's losing not the winning harms
as Jesus would have told us too*

Ferrar has gone, and the children's voices are far off now. The trees make a semi-circle, a kind of performance area, half-lit by the moon. Across it, wraiths in rags, pushing carts, dragging bundles. Behind, the outlines of mighty buildings, masts of ships, gateways, towers and spires, a solitary maypole. The smell of burning has changed to a stench. What is he witnessing? And yet he knows. This is the year when a sixth of the population of London died, over 40,000 souls, and the family left for Huntingdonshire, seeking only quarantine, but finding their spiritual home. It began with restoration of the dilapidated church (being used as a haybarn and pigsty) under the critical eye of Ferrar's formidable mother. They cleared it out, dealt with the damp and found a carpenter who knew where to find good oak for the panelling, the same oak that would be used for George Herbert's church nearby.

Begin your walk back down the avenue, where civil war
is hardly more than an unfurled leaf, a reign of peace
this twig, where poet, thinker, cunning woman, sage
are one extra inch around the waist, and the life
of the oldest arboriculturist is just some rings, a little height
and deeper roots. We never move. We make sure progress.

All things began with the squirrel and the jay. There is a day
when we emerge into the light, when we must fight the mouse
then the deer; and there is that hazy druid spell
when people dance beneath us. And even when they haul
us out to be reinterred, inverted, roots in the air,
we know it is an expression of their love and understanding.

Better than those who fell us for the sake of a fenland octagon
or cut us off at the knees to make a dependable hull
or use our arms to hold up a row of high street residences
or force us to serve as doors and floors in jogtrot planks
or carve us into intolerable shapes for sitting and sleeping.
Better than those who want to turn us into decorative panels.

Do you not see in these postures we strike the story of the earth?
The ones who preached here, trying to teach the sacred ways
of oak-lore to the growing city dwellers who had never stood
beneath our canopy before? The ones who were left here
after quarrelling over treasure, or whose heads cry out
with buried St Edmund every eleventh of September?

We carry still the prints of those who climbed to our crown
to find an answer, and those who knelt to our fungi, our moss,
to inspect the many hundred varieties of insect that we cherish.
We have inspired, and we have held back approval from those
who moved too fast and in the wrong direction. There is only
upwards, downwards, outwards. But always in the one place.

Another scene, the buildings all gone, the native trees appearing to lean back, making way for something new, a change of key. Drunken figures are playing (can it really be?) bowls, while here and there feathers poke up, quite unnoticed, sidling with the bias of the game. A sweet smell perfumes the camp. Pipes, bawdy songs, a flash of bare skin. And there goes Ferrar, holding a document, obtaining signatures from a procession of distinguished travellers and diplomats and administrators and aristocrats (that surely is the Earl of Southampton). The man is a tight-sprung machine, super-efficient, whose one concern is Virginia. Here they are loading vines to dispatch. Then mulberry trees and silkworms. More craftsmen, a headmaster, a fresh supply of priests. Now books and maps. The beginnings of a new world.

                    But here in England
                                where we are not
                                            a substitute
                    for plane
                            how everything helicopters
                                                beautifully
                      down
                            our fruits
                                    like acts of renunciation

                    We too believe
                            in renaissance art
                                            our greeny
                    flowers
                            our reddish seeds
                                        evasively smiling
                    against a rocky gorge
                                    or our limbs
                                            stretched
                    shameless
                            yet ambiguous
                                    although we would

        donate
                sweet syrup
                        if sweetly requested

        O sycamore
                acer pseudoplatanus
                            a dool tree,
a plague tree
        a posy tree
                we are
a fairy tree

                hammered
                      with Irish sixpences
a martyrs tree
                we tailspin
                      into the spring
and at every crash-site
                      the ghost
                            of an analogue schoolboy
slips
        the bark away
                to make a whistle

        How easy
                for a pseudo-plane
                        to plant its seeds

        how easy too
                for us to drop
                        our honeydew
on you and you
                and let it turn
                        to mucilage

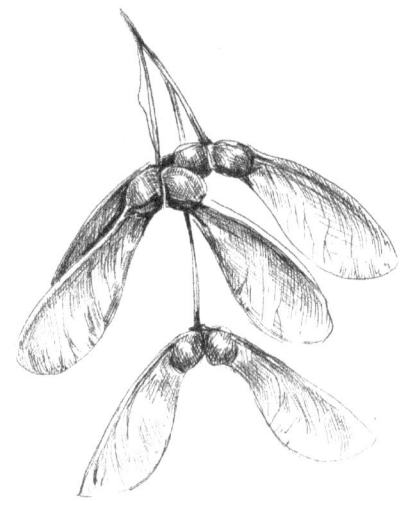

The Huntingdonshire moon has become a raw Spanish sun, and Ferrar is seen walking, younger now, walking hundreds of miles (though he never leaves Gidding, which is nowhere yet in his thoughts). He carries the rapier presented to him when he left Madrid. Nothing more. All the books he has collected have been dispatched to England, so he is free to walk and think about the future, but he is exhausted. An aged Spanish countrywoman enters with a bowl of good local sherry, offering it to him, not to drink, but to bathe his feet. The relief is obvious. But even as he thanks her, clouds move in, and he is once again lost in the mountains, desperate, praying for shelter. A black hog skitters by. He follows it and it leads him to a dubious inn, where he is closely watched from the shadows, and there is whispered negotiation as he lies down and pretends to sleep. Gradually the offstage voices work themselves up to a quarrel, hoping to draw him in and use his involvement as an excuse to rob him. But he keeps his eyes tightly shut beneath a cooling, reassuring sweet chestnut tree.

As if we were trying to   unscrew and open the earth
we torque to ourselves across   Europe, south questioning north
about yield, about harvest   lamenting the vanished hearth
missing the hiss and the spit   comparing fullness of girth

We are proud of our vision   our broad volcano-edge scope
impatient of narrow views   such as those now growing up
in the soft new plantations   that dull inward-looking group
who will not let even one   beam lead a human to hope

And the question unasked is   the oldest of chestnuts still
whether we need other trees   if we're better off single
admired in a rich man's park   Who needs your hot foreign hill
when we're dubbed Spanish Chestnut   granted a wide lawn to fill

and permitted to flourish   *a first class specimen too*
not kept to be felled for our   timber that Normandy knew
was the finest in Europe   though coppices where we grew
palings and hop-poles and beams   still survive here, the last few

No, we're torn, for our roots   go on burrowing no less
keenly than when we arrived   as colonists, Claudius
hankering still for that good   old dependency on us
in feasting and vomiting   all that we've had to erase

Spiked helmets lying in heaps   and rust from a thousand spears
though we relish those seasons   we veteran warriors
in the midst of these copses   away from the sound of wars
left by the British to rot   who prefer to play conkers

Italian music, fiddles, gut strings, performed invisibly offstage (by members of the family), as the scene is transformed to what is meant to be a botanical garden. Ferrar is still lying on the ground but now he is restless, in a high fever. Whatever it is that afflicts him, it has reached a crisis, and there can be no future if something is not done. There are herb-bushes, exotic flowers, unusual trees. We are in Padua. Doctors hurry in, leaning over their patient, tapping their lips, stroking their chins. One of them, very old, pushes his way through and insists on doing what must be done: crossing himself, he takes a sharp instrument and opens a vein, letting the Englishman's blood. As it flows, the pines on the slopes behind him shed resin tears in sympathy. They can already see Rome, Spain, Virginia, London, Little Gidding.

Few interfere so little
with what grows beneath them as
we, the Stone Pines, known by you
arboreal recusant
English – who have taken us
home to plant – as umbrellas.

Sheltering, you at least sing
like Oratorians who
know how sun can enliven
the strictest rule, and ripen
both today's fruit and the fruit
to come, as it does in Rome.

Out of sight, our table-tops
carry everything required
for flesh and blood, though only
those who have seen us in our
natural state and witnessed our
stone miracle will believe.

Meanwhile, you may gather up
remains of our other gods,
those pagan sparks confined in
discarded cones, that will flare
magic, as if they could warm
your East Anglian winter.

Low light – dawn is not far off – and a shadow procession passing, crowns, robes, footmen, ladies in waiting, their elongated shapes across the lawn. One identifiable profile: young Ferrar, joining the others on the barge. Gunfire. Flags. The sound of cheering and a band playing. Twenty oars in silhouette begin to move.

Step from the barge
and carve the way
Linnaeus showed
towards today.

The air takes up
his instrument:
a name, a scale,
a humming scent.

These little hearts
in lowland shade
prepare their ticker-
tape parade.

This trunk tries out
its sounding board
to celebrate
the iron word

or holds its shield
against assault
from those who say
you are at fault.

My bark knows how
to heal a bite.
Unpeel these peaceful
thoughts I write.

I lay this mat
beneath your feet.
I make you nectar,
green and sweet.

Carve what you like.
Your way is free.
But only under
the linden tree.

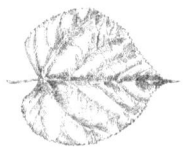

Dawn at last, and the final scene looks for all the world like Cambridge, limes in leaf in the colleges, along the backs and in fenny corners blackthorn (or may?) flowering, the air full of pollen. Spring has arrived, and sunshine. Strangely, he feels more rooted than ever, though there is little now to identify Little Gidding as such, except the church, and the tomb in front. But the whole area once home to the community has been given over to a fair, such a mixture of types and styles and behaviours. He is swept up in the mood of the participants, who are thronging around a single hawthorn trunk, trailing ribbons.

The white witch with her lipstick and her teenage spells
   leaves the street, takes a ribbon, and dances

The maker of cogwheels, pallid, mechanical, bored
   leaves the street, takes a ribbon, and dances

The good woman of the department of unfunded prehistory
   leaves the street, takes a ribbon, and dances

The gilded model, painted in poisonous tongues
   leaves the street, takes a ribbon, and dances

The verger's foster-daughter in her peacock costume
   leaves the street, takes a ribbon, and dances

The ornamental twins, shimmering, shaking with the giggles,
   leave the street, take a ribbon, are dancing

The dairy employee, her pail, her churn, her yoke
   leaves the street, takes a ribbon, and dances

The queen of the bogs, has put on clogs, jewellery
   leaves the street, takes a ribbon, and dances

The cricket widow, celebrating her maiden century
   leaves the street, takes a ribbon, and dances

The crack addict, murderous, frothing with pink
   leaves the street, takes a ribbon, and dances

The long-term resident, Eve, her whitening fall,
   leaves the street, takes a ribbon, and dances

The one who arrived at Christmas is still refusing
   to leave the street, take a ribbon, or dance

And there is Ferrar again, even younger now, beardless, but recognisable and evidently tempted by the dancing. He resists, walks away – though this brings him closer to his silent observer – and sits thoughtfully on a low branch of yew, next to a silver birch.

Y

Forwards and backwards are the same.
 He's yet to realise that's the case.
Although he's guessed it's all a game
 of patience, not a human race.

B

You know about patience, certainly,
 and how an arrow from your bow
will never hit a bullseye, halving
 the distance till the atoms show.

Y

And you could teach him a thing or two
 about how to bend and how to give
and how to mend the poor man's shoe
 and live where others fear to live.

B

A graveyard wouldn't be my choice,
   but nor do I have that special touch
when it comes to terminal advice
   which seems to please you both so much.

Y

It brings me joy that he takes heed
   how life and death must grow as one
like toxins round my precious seed
   or gamma rays within the sun.

B

I have to say I'm pleased he knows
   I write and can be written on
and has forgiven me the blows
   when teachers had their fascist fun.

Y

We know that he will make his mark
   in forests far from yours and mine.
But may he dream of my rough bark
   in Holland or above the Rhine.

B

And may he see my flakes of white
   in Italy and Spain and when
he comes to London, as the night-
   mare plague begins to bite again.

Y

In Little Gidding may he know
the yew-tree

B

and the silver birch.

Y & B

And notice us and how we grow
as he walks by each day to church.

He almost says *amen*. But immediately it is evident that the performance space has said it for him. It is deserted. He is alone at Little Gidding. He remembers that his staff have no idea where he has vanished to. As he turns to begin the walk back to the Travelodge, he becomes aware of what is in his hand. A birch twig with catkins, and a sprig of yew. He lays them on Nicholas Ferrar's tomb and sets off.

John Greening was born in 1954 and since *Westerners* in 1982, he has published over twenty collections of poetry, most recently *The Silence* (Carcanet, 2019), which features his long poem about Jean Sibelius, and three pamphlets: *Achill Island Tagebuch* (Redfoxpress, 2019), *Europa's Flight* (New Walk Editions, 2019), and *Moments Musicaux* (Poetry Salzburg Review, 2020). Other books include guides to poets and poetry (Elizabethans, WW1 Poets, Yeats, Edward Thomas, Hardy), together with editions of Geoffrey Grigson and Edmund Blunden, whose memoir *Undertones of War* he edited for OUP in 2015. His new selection of Iain Crichton Smith's poetry, *Deer on the High Hills*, has just appeared from Carcanet. There have been several anthologies, notably *Accompanied Voices: Poets on Composers from Thomas Tallis to Arvo Pärt* (Boydell, 2015), *Ten Poems about Sheds* (Candlestick, 2018) and the forthcoming *Hollow Palaces* (a selection of modern country-house poems, with Kevin Gardner, Liverpool UP, 2021). In 2016 he collaborated with Penelope Shuttle on *Heath* (Nine Arches), and earlier in 2021 there was a shared collection of 'postcard sonnets' exchanged with poet Stuart Henson (*a Post Card to*, Red Squirrel Press). Musical collaborations include contributions to Roderick Williams's Schubert Project with composer Cecilia McDowall, and a libretto about the Niagara Falls for the Dunedin Consort. John Greening has reviewed for the *TLS* since the 1990s and his collected essays and reviews, *Vapour Trails*, were published by Shoestring Press in 2020. There has also been a memoir of the two years he and his wife spent in Egypt: *Threading a Dream: a Poet on the Nile* (Gatehouse, 2016). He has won the Bridport Prize and received a Cholmondeley Award from the Society of Authors. Until recently he was RLF Writing Fellow at Newnham College, Cambridge.

Acknowledgments are due to the editors of the following publications in which extracts from *The Giddings* have appeared:

The Long Poem Magazine, Quadrant (Aus), *The Hudson Review* (USA).

Thanks to the trustees of Hawthornden International Writers' Retreat for a residency in 2017, during which *The Giddings* was composed.

The illustrations are by **Rosie Greening**, a London-based artist who specialises in faces and places. When she isn't drawing and painting she writes children's books for a small publisher.

Lightning Source UK Ltd.
Milton Keynes UK
UKHW050807250421
382550UK00007B/44